A Flow of Encouragement For

The Married Couple

S.D. Horton

A Flow of Encouragement For
The Married Couple

Copyright © 2007 by S.D. Horton
ISBN: 978-1-4303-1720-3

Cover design by S.D. Horton & The Harris Marketing Group

Editorial assistance by Cheryl Horton

A Flow of Encouragement
For
The Married Couple

Contents

Dedication

I dedicate all of my writings to my beautiful wife, Cheryl, who has always supported me and has been one of the main reasons why I pursue my dreams. To my children DeAundre, Jasmine, & Jalen who have always been my inspiration. To my parents and brothers who are always there for me with their support and prayers. A **<u>very</u>** special thanks to my life coach and mentor, Dr. Mikel Brown & his wife Debra, for continuously pushing me into living my dream. Words cannot express how my family and I appreciate the mark you have left on our lives. Thank you so much! And finally, to everyone else who have supported me throughout my whole life. Trust me, I know who you are. Thank you for all you have done.

Special Thanks

Special thanks to the following individuals/families who gave their financial seeds to enable me to accomplish my dream in writing this series.

Kim Clark
Tarik & Lourie Booze
Brian & Cynthia Harris
Kerwin & Kim Dewberry
Darius & Priscilla Jones
Harry & Brandi Daniels

Foreword

The *Living Waters*: *A Flow of Encouragement* series is designed to provide a continuous flow of encouraging words to those who are in need of a "pick-me-up". Life presents many opportunities to everyone, but it also presents problems, discouragement, and failure. You do not have to go through life aimlessly! *A Flow of Encouragement* is here to show you the light at the end of the tunnel. Regardless of the negatives presented in life, or even opposition from people, you can still be a success.

S.D. Horton
Author

A Flow of Encouragement For

The Married Couple

"Wow! I'm married now! I love my spouse so much, that I would jump off a cliff for them." Sound familiar? The sparkling cider may still be bubbling over the neck of the bottle; you have just placed a layer of your wedding cake in the freezer; or maybe your house still has rose petals perfectly aligned along the hallway leading to the bedroom. These signs point to the fact that you are finally married! You have found your "soul mate" and ready to do anything and everything for them.

God has finally answered your prayers and you are ready to prove to everyone that your marriage will be the perfect marriage. If you have been married for less than a year, you may be asking within yourself, "What can possibly go wrong?" or "Our marriage is great. Is it possible for it to get any better?" The answers are "everything" and "yes", respectively. Please consider the following as you continue to travel into the unknown world of marriage.

1

One + One = Two

A Drop of Encouragement

Your marriage will be as good as the two of you want it to be!

1

One + One = Two

Marriage involves two people: a husband **and** a wife. In other words, you are not the only one in the house. Your concerns have now become your spouse's concerns and vice-versa. In a perfect world, you and your spouse would be able to read each other's minds. Since we are not in a perfect world, reading each other's minds is virtually impossible. The next best thing is communication. The anatomy definition for communication is "an opening or connecting passage between two structures". In relation to marriage, communication is a vehicle used by **both** parties to bridge the gap caused by unfamiliarity. Both of you have many different dreams and ambitions, and until you establish a balance through communication, the two of you will never become unified.

Humility is required to develop a great balance through communication. Although two separate ideas are presented in your marriage, it is imperative that you get on the same sheet of music. One of the ways you could ensure that this happens is to weed out the things that are not needed and keep the things that are needed. In other words, if your ideas will hinder the overall objective in the marriage, toss them out of the window. This takes humility. Sometimes it's difficult to cease in doing something you've probably done all of your single, adult life. If you realize how detrimental it would be in your marriage, you should have no problem with getting rid of it. Once again, remember that there are two people in your house now. Start off on the right foot my humbling yourselves and considering the marriage as a whole.

Having confidence in each other is important to your marriage. What spouse (in their right mind) wants to live with someone who is not confident in them? As a married couple, the both of you must develop a hunger to pursue the knowledge of what it takes to trust and have confidence in each other. Remember, you're in this thing together. If one is trying harder than the other, there's an imbalance. Have a meeting with each other and decide what steps the two of you are going to take together in order to establish and maintain a healthy trust relationship. You must know that it's going to take time and diligence, so don't give up. The journey may be long and tiresome, but it will be worth your time. Just as a sprinter knows that dedication is needed to win the gold medal, you too must understand that it takes patience to obtain your ultimate goal.

2

Let the 2 = 1

A Drop of Encouragement

*Working as one in your marriage is more effective
than working separately as two!*

2

Let the 2 = 1

Once you have "somewhat" figured each other out, you will then begin to realize that the two of you are actually forming into one. When dealing with situations in a marriage, working as one is much more powerful than working as two. Having two visions will cause division, but having a unified vision will cause prosperity and growth. A scripture in the Bible says "a house divided against itself cannot stand." What a true and profound statement! Beach volleyball is a sport that's usually played as a two-man (or two-woman) team. During a match, it is imperative that the setter successfully sets the ball to his/her partner in order to increase the chances of attaining a point for the team. If the ball is set too far to the left or right, the partner may not be able to effectively spike the ball on the opposite side of the net. If the two-man team don't soon come together as **one** to resolve their issues, a loss would be inevitable for them. Likewise, unless the two of you come together and unite your visions, division will be inevitable and growth will not be attained.

One of the most difficult areas for couples to function as one is in the financial department. Although it's one of the hardest, it's not impossible! Many couples choose to maintain separate bank accounts, while others decide to establish joint accounts. Whatever you have decided, ensure that the communication line remains open. Remember, your main objective is to become one. Finances, or the lack thereof, have been used as the scapegoat for the demise of many marriages. Don't let this happen to you. Talk with your spouse and consider the advantages and disadvantages of establishing joint accounts. The key, once again, is communication. Establish a budget, decide who's going to pay what particular bill, etc. Believe it or not, these are key in developing and maintaining a healthy marriage.

As you're steadily forming into one, don't ever entertain the "go sleep on the couch" idea. Your spouse is too precious for you to allow an argument to separate you for even one night. This is where communication comes into play. Do not be afraid to tell your spouse how they hurt you. Discuss the disagreement with each other and allow the healing process to take place. I can recall one night that I was upset with my wife. She didn't send me to the couch, but I chose to go there anyway! I felt as if I needed space and time away from her. While on the couch, I was thinking about her the whole time. I was still mad, but she was on my mind. I then realized that it was unfruitful for me to be on the couch. From that day on, I don't go to the couch as a result of an argument or disagreement with my spouse. We have learned that we need to settle things before they try to separate us.

Realizing the two of you are becoming one is also helpful in making important decisions. We tend to lean more toward our own feelings without considering the feelings of our spouse. When we do that, we become close-minded and stubborn. You're not the only one with an idea! Your spouse is just as important as you are in providing ideas for decision making. Allow them to suggest things to you and you may soon realize that your idea was not as good as you thought it would be. Why? As the saying goes, there's more than one way to skin a cat! With math being my favorite subject in high school, I was always fascinated at the many ways you could solve one particular equation. There were various methods, but the same agenda. Likewise, there are different ideas brought to the table in a discussion, but the objective is still to work as one.

3

Love *vs.* Purpose

A Drop of Encouragement

Love may have brought you together, but purpose is going to keep you together!

3

Love *vs.* Purpose

As a married couple, you will soon realize that love <u>alone</u> will not sustain any marriage. Love may have brought your significant other to you, but purpose will keep that spouse sustained and always wanting more from the relationship. Many divorced couples can tell you that if they could turn back the hands of time, they would have determined the purpose of their marriage. Many of them would also say, foolishly (in some cases), that they would have not married their former spouse had they known what they know now. Well, when you depend only on love to determine the success of your marriage, you will be most miserable!

You will also realize that the excitement level you once had for your spouse will not maintain its intensity if you do not discover and begin to walk according to your purpose. I can vividly recall the first time I intensely laid eyes on my wife. It was what many would call, "love at first sight." But I would not phrase it in that manner. I definitely saw purpose. I may not have fully understood it at the time, but I did know that if we were to get married, it would not be based on love alone. During our time of getting to know one another, my spouse and I developed a healthy friendship. We went to church together, we played board games together, and we went on many dates. As a matter of fact, since the day we started to date, we "hung out" with each other every day of the week for 4 months. I believe the streak would have continued if I did not have to leave for a short military school assignment. Two months later, we were married. One thing we **did not** take part in during our courtship was pre-marital sex. We understood that we had purpose for being together.

I encourage you to have a meeting with your spouse on a frequent basis. First of all, determine the purpose for which you are married. Second, make a vow to one another that you will do everything you need to do to make sure that the purpose will be fulfilled! Next, agree that you would separate yourselves from anybody who would try to create a gap between the two of you. This includes, but is not limited to close friends, family members, enemies, and outsiders. Finally, because you know that walking in your purpose requires dedication, concentration, drive, and commitment, you and your spouse must agree that both of you will be diligent in protecting your purpose from ultimate failure. Now sit back, relax, and watch how successful your marriage will be!

4

Between the Sheets

A Drop of Encouragement

Although sex is good, it's still not the best answer to marital problems!

4

Between the Sheets

Along with finances, sex is another area in marriage where couples find it hard to agree as one. You may ask, "Why? Sex is as easy as boiling an egg!" Well, many couples don't consider the activities that happen before and after the "do" is done.

Too often, sex is used as a bandage to cover the real problems in a marriage. What's the most popular way to make up after an argument? Sex! What's the easiest way for a married man or woman to disguise their lust problem? Sex! Many may think that lust is an innocent problem, but they're wrong! You could be physically making love to your spouse, but mentally be with another partner from your past, which we will discuss in another chapter. You could mentally be with an actor/actress you've fantasized about all of your life. You could even be thinking about a sex scene in a movie or pornography film. Either way, your thoughts are not properly focused! Sex is designed for enjoyment (and/or procreation) with the spouse you're married to. Don't contaminate that enjoyment by prostituting it! Imagine how beautiful and exciting making love would be if it's just the two of you.

Although sex is good, it's still not the best answer to many of the issues married couples deal with. Your spouse deserves better! He/she don't need you to dump all of your garbage on them in the form of sex! Don't ever use sex as a substitute for talking. It may gratify you for the time, but after the love-making is over, the issue will still be there. I've known married couples that had great sex lives, but the marriage still ended. They may have thought, "as long as the sex continues to be good, all of the other things will just fall in line." This couldn't be any further away from the truth. Sex is not a substitute! It is an entity of its own.

Sex doesn't start with the actual physical action. It starts with what's commonly known as foreplay. Don't misunderstand me….there are times when "a little dab will do", but not for the most part. My life coach once explained to me that how I present something to someone is just as important as the item I'm presenting. He used food as an example. Having a steak and mashed potatoes as a meal is good on any given day, but if that same meal is presented on a garbage lid, it becomes less desirable. Why? Because of the presentation! The meal may have looked good, but it was presented to me in a disrespectful manner.

In the same way, how you present yourself to your spouse speaks volumes about how you feel about him/her. During foreplay, if I would dare approach my wife like she's a piece of meat, the response I receive will be a memorable one! On the other hand, if I caress her, rub my fingers through her hair, and tell her how much I truly love her and that I'm going to take my time with her, I have just promised her that she's going to have the time of her life, and we're both going to enjoy it together! I personally know that I'm the best man that has ever stepped into my wife's life! I'm confident in this because I'm not in competition with any other man! All that I need, she freely gives to me and all that I have is reserved only for her!

I realize that my marriage is healthy because during conversation time, we converse with enjoyment; during dinnertime, we eat with enjoyment; and during intercourse time, we're making love between the sheets with enjoyment.

5

Healing From Past Relationships

A Drop of Encouragement

*You will not progress in your current marriage if you
do not receive healing from your past relationships!*

5

Healing from Past Relationships

Let's face it! The two of you have both experienced some trying times if you were ever involved in previous relationships. The past can truly haunt you if you don't know how to be rescued from it. You must learn to identify the strategic tactics from your past that are designed to annihilate your marriage. These tactics are designed to destroy the love, commitment, and trust levels in your current relationship.

Comparing past lovers with your current spouse will be a detriment to your marriage. If you allow old feelings to linger in your heart, it could cause a great downfall in your marriage. The downfall may not happen in a few days, or even a few months. It could be a few years before it rears its ugly head. You must first acknowledge that the feelings still exist. Acknowledging your feelings does not show weakness; it actually shows strength. It also shows that you are willing to expose those feelings and not hide them. Anything that's hidden will eventually be revealed, and most of the time it's revealed at the most inopportune time.

During my years of counseling couples that are engaged or already married, I've always stressed the need to be open with your feelings, even if they're for someone else. It is easier to deal with a problem in its early stages than to wait until it takes root and begin to affect other areas of your life. Being an experienced wood-hauler, I understand that the strength of a tree is in its roots. These roots are designed to provide water and nutrients to the tree for its survival and growth. Once the roots are established, they begin to spread horizontally and the tree becomes stabilized and is able to live many years. However, if you cut off these roots at the trunk, the tree will die because it has lost its life source. Likewise, if you don't eradicate those past feelings, they will be like cancer and spread throughout your marriage. Every area of your marriage will be in danger of being infected!

I recall the time when I decided to tell my wife about an area of darkness I allowed to fester in my life. I realized that I had to tell her because this area of darkness was affecting my marriage. I realized that the darkness had to be brought to light so that the healing process could start. Once I told her, I felt a sense of freedom. She didn't judge, or even criticize me. She listened to me and she was patient with me. Now, that area of darkness is not a problem to me because it has been exposed! That night was the start of a new beginning for our marriage. Now, I don't hide anything from my wife.

A year or so after that night, I can recall an occurrence that happened while I was away from my family on a temporary military assignment. While at that particular assignment, I came in contact with a female with whom I had a relationship with 11 years prior. It was a very awkward moment for the both of us. After we talked for a couple of minutes, I went outside, called my wife and told her about this occurrence. In the past, I would have hidden this from my spouse to perhaps seize an opportunity to sexually reacquaint myself with the young lady. However, I understood that the love for my spouse was, and still is greater than anything else presented to me from an outside source! As the song goes, "Ain't no woman like the one I got"!

Don't allow your past to come back to haunt you! Deal with it! You have the power to allow or disallow the things in your past to cause problems in your marriage. Communicate with your spouse. Let your spouse know how you feel. It's better to do it now than in divorce court!

6

Spend a Little Time with Me

A Drop of Encouragement

A marriage that has balance is a healthy marriage!

6

Spend a Little Time with Me

Your favorite football team is playing in the Super Bowl and your wife, who's not an avid football fan, wants to spend some time with you. What do you do? Your favorite sitcom is on and your husband, who's not a big fan of sitcoms, wants to go on a walk around the block with you. What do you do? Well, if I had the answer to this, I'll be a billionaire! I may not have the right answer for everyone, but I do, however, have the following suggestions.

The ability to negotiate, or compromise, is an art that many married couples have not learned to master. A marriage that has balance is a healthy marriage. Being able to recognize the desires of your spouse will earn you much kudos. Personally, I'm not a big fan of emotional movies, or what's commonly called "chick flicks". My wife wanted me to watch this particular "chick flick" with her, but I constantly postponed the movie night. Well, on one of my days off from work, I decided to watch this movie. Needless to say, I enjoyed it. I even shed a tear or two. Once I told her about it, she said, "I told you it was good. You could have watched it with me". Now, I look forward to having movie night with my wife, regardless of the type of movie.

Before we got married, my wife knew that I was a devout baseball fan. She hated the sport, but she learned how to master the art of compromise years before I did. Whenever my favorite team was on television, she would occasionally sit down and watch some of the game with me. Eventually, I took her to a live game and she enjoyed herself. Now, she sits with me to watch the entire game on television. When I'm away from the house, she calls to give me the score. She gets just as excited or frustrated as I get during the game. It's awesome!

We have both learned how to negotiate with each other. We enjoy spending time together. As a married couple, you must spend time together. One of the biggest mistakes a lot of seasoned married couples make is deciding to not spend as much time with each other as they did earlier in their marriage. These days, you don't find too many married couples going to the movies or out to dinner without their kids. They would say, "We don't have time to go out to dinner", or "it cost money to pay for a baby-sitter". Well, paying for a baby-sitter is worth it. You want to continue to invest in your marriage. You want your marriage to continue to grow. As my life coach would say, anything that's stagnant will begin to stink. You don't want your marriage to stink. You want your marriage to have life. You want single people to see your marriage as an example of how they want their marriage to be. Don't ever slack off in spending time together. Don't ever put your spouse in the position of having to beg for you to spend some quality time with them. It's better to spend too much time than not enough time.

According to a recent Pittsburg study, spending time with your spouse might be good for your heart. It develops a sense of familiarity, trust, and commitment. I'm a firm believer in designating your spouse as your best friend. You don't have a lot of anxiety when you can trust the one you're living with. Because my wife trusts me so much, I walk around with a sense of pride or with a chip on my shoulder knowing that she can depend on me for anything. Likewise, I don't have to worry if my wife is cheating on me because she's open and honest with me. For that, I trust her! She has proven herself time and time again. I have no reason to doubt her, like I have not given her a reason for her to doubt me. We continue to spend quality time together. We have such a strong bond together that no one is able to separate.

7

Let's Stay Together!

A Drop of Encouragement

What God has joined together, let no man separate!

7

Let's Stay Together!

My wife and I made a huge and bold decision when we became engaged. We decided that this was it! No need to look for another because we're with each other for the rest of our lives! It may have been a bold declaration to some, but to us it's the only way to believe! First of all, we both understand that God brought us together. The Bible says that what God has joined together, let no man separate. In other words, we totally depend on God's strength in our marriage and lives.

Second, we are both on the same path in life. Once, I heard a good friend say something that really should be heard by every single person desiring to become married. He said, in a nutshell, that while running your race (in life), it's important to stay your course. Sure, you may desire a spouse, but your aspiration is to have a spouse who's running the same race and speed with you. If you deviate (look back), you begin to slow down and settle for what's handed to you. But, if you remain diligent, you have no desire for what's behind you! You're only concerned with what's ahead for you. The things behind have already been trampled over by your feet, but the things ahead of you have yet to be experienced.

Having the desire to stay together is not the norm in today's society. The divorce rate has really sky-rocketed! Many couples come to the decision that it's easier to give up than it is to stick it out. You see couples who have been married for over 20 years decide to suddenly call it quits because of the fear of getting old with that spouse. It seems as if love and purpose have been replaced with hate and dishonesty. Regardless, however, of the escalating divorce & separation rate and despite the large number of infidelity cases, you do not have to fall into the same traps! Your marriage has the potential to be a success, but it's up to you.

One of the things my wife and I do to enhance our marriage is have question/answer sessions. We ask each other how we feel about each other. We also ask each other to grade our various components of marriage (communication, intimacy, etc.) on a scale from 1 to 10. While this may sound redundant on the surface, it actually keeps our foundation alive and strong. One day, I called my wife and, out of the blue, asked her how she felt about me. She simply said "I love and enjoy you because you bear with me and teach me things." Those words were a delight to my ears. My wife is not as spontaneous as I am, but she has her moments. At that time, those words made my day!

You must strongly desire to make this marriage work. Never allow situations to dictate how you feel about each other. Always encourage one another. Always have the mindset that you will always stay together, no matter what comes against you!

Conclusion

Congratulations married couple! You have entered into a covenant that is going to take the two of you to sustain. Remember, you are a team now. Don't allow anyone or anything from your past to come in and destroy the covenant you have promised to keep.

About the Author

S.D. Horton is a successful businessman, author, and religious leader in a local church. He was born in Columbus, GA and raised in Talbotton, GA. He is an Air Force veteran and currently resides in Alamogordo, NM with his wife and children.

Autograph